Ryder School Library
Cobleskill, New York

Bird Mania

By Ed and Ruth Radlauer

85-410

AN ELK GROVE BOOK

CHILDRENS PRESS, CHICAGO

Photo credits:
   Robin Radlauer, pages 8, 9
   Rolf Zillmer, page 21

3 9014 30003 4176

Library of Congress Cataloging in Publication Data

Radlauer, Edward.
   Bird mania

   (Mania books)
   "An Elk Grove book."
   SUMMARY: Introduces a variety of birds such as macaws, peacocks, flamingos, owls, swans, and pelicans.
   1. Birds—Juvenile literature. [1. Birds]
I. Radlauer, Ruth Shaw, joint author. II. Title.
QL676.2.R32   598   80-21833
ISBN 0-516-07782-1

Copyright © 1981 by Regensteiner Publishing Enterprises, Inc.
All rights reserved. Published simultaneously in Canada.
Printed in the United States of America.

1 2 3 4 5 6 7 8 9 10 11 12 13 14 15 R 87 86 85 84 83 82 81

A RADLAUER
Mania Book

**CREATED FOR CHILDRENS PRESS BY
*RADLAUER PRODUCTIONS INCORPORATED**

Bird mania?

Yes, this is bird mania.
A pigeon makes a good pet.

A pigeon is a good pet bird.
And a green parrot
is a good pet, too.

You can talk to a
green pet parrot.

Your pet may be a macaw.

Can a macaw talk to a macaw?

Chickens are birds.
Some chickens eat—

—and some chickens sing.
Chickens sing?

Do peacocks sing?

No, a peacock shows its blue and green tail feathers.

A flamingo shows pink
or white feathers.

A flamingo can sleep standing on one foot.

When it's not standing asleep on one foot, you can see a flamingo's little yellow eye.

And when an owl is not sleeping, you can see its big yellow eyes and short bill.

Some bills are short
and some are long.

Some bills are sharp.

And some bird bills are sharp and long—

—or sharp, long, and strong.

If you like white,
you may like swans.

White swans like the water.

Pelicans are water birds—

—and pelicans live near the water.

Some birds like to fly.

Some like to fly
and some like to talk.

Water birds like to swim.

Water birds swim, but ostriches like to race. Ostriches like to race?

Bird mania?

Yes, it's bird mania.

Bird Words

page

 4 bird, mania
 5 yes, this, is, a, pigeon, makes, good, pet
 6 and, green, parrot, too
 7 you, can, talk, to
 8 your, may, be, macaw
 9
10 chickens, are, birds, some, eat
11 sing
12 do, peacocks
13 no, peacock, shows, its, blue, tail, feathers
14 flamingo, pink, or, white
15 sleep, standing, on, one, foot
16 when, it's, not, asleep, see, flamingo's, little, yellow, eye
17 an, owl, sleeping, big, eyes, short, bill
18 bills, long
19 sharp
20
21 strong
22 if, like, white, swans
23 the, water
24 pelicans
25 live, near
26 fly
27
28 swim
29 ostriches, race
30
31

Date Due